D1062313

ROSIE'S
WALK

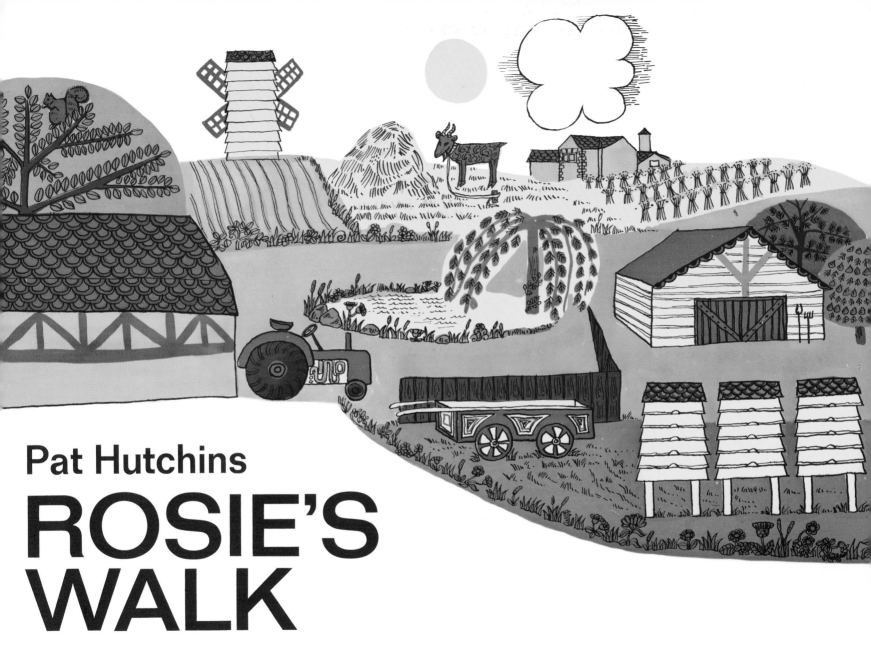

Pat Hutchins

ROSIE'S
WALK

HARCOURT BRACE & COMPANY
Orlando   Atlanta   Austin   Boston   San Francisco   Chicago   Dallas   New York
Toronto   London

This edition is published by special arrangement with Macmillan Publishing
Company, a division of Macmillan, Inc.

Grateful acknowledgment is made to Macmillan Publishing Company, a
division of Macmillan, Inc. for permission to reprint *Rosie's Walk* by Pat
Hutchins. Copyright © 1968 by Patricia Hutchins.

Printed in the United States of America

ISBN 0-15-302113-6

4 5 6 7 8 9 10   035   97 96 95

For
Wendy
and
Stephen

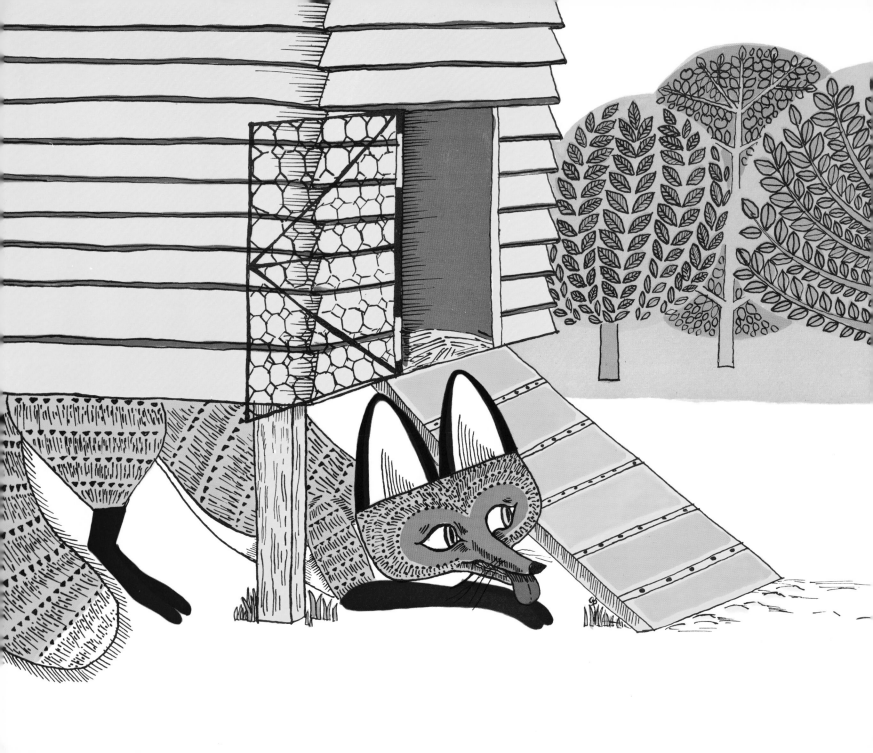

Rosie the hen went for a walk

across the yard

around

the

pond

over the haystack

past the mill

through the fence

under the beehives

and
got back
in time
for dinner.